Contents

The Dolphin Family

The animal that most people think of as a 'dolphin' is the bottlenose dolphin, *Tursiops truncatus*. The bottlenose dolphin, though, is only one member of a rather large family of dolphins. The word 'family' in scientific nomenclature describes a group of animals that are relatively closely related.

The term 'species' is the most specific level of description there is, besides having individuals of the same species. Humans are all one species, *Homo sapiens*, and our close relatives are the so-called 'non-human primates' and include animals like chimpanzees.

The word 'cetacea' is derived from the Latin word *cetus*, which means 'whale', and *cetacean* is a sub-order that contains all of the whales and dolphins. While many people think of the difference between whales and dolphins being their size, with whales being large and dolphins small, scientists categorize them not into 'big' or 'small' but as 'toothed' or 'baleen'. The toothed whales, or *odontocetes*, have real teeth, whereas the baleen whales, or *mysticetes*, filter their food with frayed plates of baleen, which is similar in its composition to finger nails.

There are large and small representatives of both of these groups,

SPINNER DOLPHIN

The dolphin family or Delphinidae *is the largest of the marine mammals with about 65 species. The dolphins are followed closely by the beaked whales or* Ziphiidae, *though we know much less about them compared to the dolphins. Members of the dolphin family inhabit almost every habitat in the ocean, from tropical to arctic, and some, such as killer whales, range throughout the oceans.*

BOTTLENOSE DOLPHIN (left)

SPINNER DOLPHIN

Despite having very different markings in adulthood, spinner and spotted dolphins are closely related, and share the same taxonomic family, Delphinidae. Their pointed 'beak' and erect, sickle-shaped dorsal fin separate these species from porpoises, which may occur in the same locality.

ATLANTIC SPOTTED DOLPHINS (right)

and the terms 'whale' and 'dolphin' don't necessarily tell us anything about size or even taxonomic group.

The familiar bottlenose dolphin has many 'cousins', a term used to describe species that are within the same taxonomic family, specifically the dolphin family, or *delphinidae*. The delphinid family includes all of the dolphins, from the tiny Hector's dolphin all the way up to the mighty killer whale which, strictly speaking, is a dolphin. There are several things that distinguish dolphins from the closely related porpoises, such as the shape of their rostrum or snout. Dolphins tend to have elongated rostrums, thus the name 'bottlenose' for our well-known species. Porpoises, on the other hand, tend to have shortened, more rounded rostrums. Another difference is the shape of the teeth – dolphin's teeth are cone shaped while porpoise's teeth are shaped like a spade.

There are over 60 members of the dolphin family. The following gives you a feeling for the breadth and diversity of this, the largest family of cetaceans.

Oceanic Dolphins

Most of the ocean lies far from shore where the water is quite deep. In this oceanic environment many species of dolphins live their lives, never coming within sight of shore. One of the challenges faced by dolphins in any environment is how to pursue and capture their prey, and in these open-water surroundings dolphins have no natural barriers except the surface against which to corner their prey. Not surprisingly, one of the primary foraging techniques that has been observed in these animals is to corral large schools of prey into a mass near the surface. The dolphins then take turns swimming through the prey school to catch their food while the others continue to swim around the school to keep it concentrated. Oceanic dolphins are often found in large groups, with thousands of animals in a group not uncommon.

The term 'pelagic' is derived from the Greek *pelagos*, which means 'the sea', so any species that lives its life far from the coast is described using this term. One of these species is the rough-toothed dolphin, *Steno bredanensis*. Rough-toothed dolphins get their name from the fine ridges that run down the enamel of their teeth. These dolphins are about the same size as bottlenose dolphins, though relatively little is known about them, and much of what is known, only comes from studying animals that strand themselves on the beach.

SHORT-SNOUTED SPINNER DOLPHIN
Dolphins come in many shapes and sizes, from the relatively tiny franciscana and Hector's dolphins at less than 5 ft (1.5 m) in length to the mighty killer whale with males reaching 30 ft (9 m)! Despite this wide variety in sizes, the dolphin family shares common traits such as elongated rostrums, at least when compared to porpoises, and all dolphins have conical-shaped teeth, whereas the porpoises all have spade-shaped teeth.

COMMON DOLPHINS (left)

PANTROPICAL SPOTTED DOLPHINS

Spotted and spinner dolphins normally live in groups, as do most oceanic dolphins. Group living provides advantages of protection from predators and in the constant search for patchy schools of prey. But this togetherness sometimes comes at a price, because large numbers may drown at the same time if they become trapped in fishing nets.

SPINNER DOLPHINS (right)

Another fascinating pelagic species is the pantropical spotted dolphin, *Stenella attenuata*. Spotted dolphins often live in enormous groups of hundreds or even thousands of individuals. They feed on many different species of fishes, but are better known for their involvement in one of the largest human fishing operations. Pantropical spotted dolphins are one of the two species that are most commonly caught in the tuna fishery. Though the relationship between tuna and dolphins is not fully understood, schools of highly desirable tuna can often be found swimming below these massive groups of dolphins. The fishermen realized this and so would 'set' their nets around schools of dolphins and then purse in the bottom of the net to trap the tuna. Meanwhile, the dolphins were also enclosed, and when the nets were completely closed to collect the fish, many dolphins were killed because they were either trapped in the net or below other animals and could not get to the surface to breathe.

Animals that are caught that are not the target species are known as 'by-catch'. Before the international awareness of this problem, tens of thousands of dolphins were killed each year in this fishery, but now that number is significantly lower as many measures have been implemented to reduce the by-catch of dolphins.

Another pelagic species that is commonly known as a 'whale' but is

LONG-FINNED PILOT WHALES

Pilot whales and four other species of small whales, including killer and false killer whales, form a distinct group of cetaceans formerly called 'blackfish'. Currently classified as Delphinidae, and regarded as closely related to dolphins, these whales differ from their smaller cousins in size, behavior and appearance.

SOUTHERN RIGHT WHALE DOLPHINS (right)

Uniquely among dolphins, the two species of right whale dolphins have no dorsal fin.

actually another large member of the dolphin family is the long-finned pilot whale, *Globicephala melas*. There is some interesting history associated with this, as well as the short-finned species. The common name 'pilot whale' came about because these whales often swim in front of ships for extended periods of time, giving the impression that they are leading or 'piloting' the ship. Many cetaceans will swim in the pressure wave created by the bow of a ship, so called 'bow riding'. The animals actually enjoy a free ride, being pushed along by the bow wave, a bit like surfing! So, pilot whales do bow ride, but they also travel along with ships for many miles outside of the bow wave as if to guide the ship on its travels.

Pilot Whales also have an unusual common name associated with them. Particularly in the Caribbean, pilot whales were known as 'blackfish', most likely because of their jet-black pigment. Pilot whales live in very tight family units that are again focused on matrilineal lines, a fact learned primarily from groups of whales that strand on the beach or are taken as by-catch.

The northern and southern right whale dolphins, *Lissodelphis borealis* and *peronii*, are unique in several ways. Again, do not be confused by the common name, which in this case has both 'whale' and 'dolphin'; these are definitely dolphins. They were probably dubbed 'right whale' dolphins because of one of their primary features, or rather the lack of a feature. These dolphins do not have a dorsal fin. One would think that the dorsal fin is an important piece of anatomy for cetaceans, especially considering the size of some of them. The dorsal fins of male killer whales can reach almost 6 ft 6 in (2 m). The right whale, one of the baleen whales, also lacks a dorsal fin, but both species appear to function just fine without them. The northern right whale dolphin lives in the north Pacific while the southern species inhabits the southern ocean. Right whale dolphins are medium sized and exclusively pelagic.

One of the smallest delphinids, the hourglass dolphin, *Lagenorhynchus cruciger*, is also one of the oceanic dolphins. As the name suggests, one of their most noticeable features is an hourglass-shaped patch of lighter color along their sides. These dolphins reach only about 6 ft (1.8 m) in length as adults, much smaller than the white-beaked dolphin, which is also a member of the same genus, *Lagenorhynchus*. They are beautiful to see in the ocean as that hourglass patch flashes at you as they swim past. To see them, though, you would have to travel quite far south towards the Antarctic, because they are truly polar, usually staying south of 450° S latitude.

Coastal Dolphins

Perhaps the most well known dolphin species are those that spend at least part of their lives in the coastal oceans. First, a word about what is considered to be 'coastal'; oceanographers often refer to coastal as those waters extending out to the edge of the continental shelf, depending on the depth. Whatever the demarcation, the dolphins discussed here as coastal are those that spend much of their lives in coastal waters. As with the river dolphins, the coastal species possess adaptations to their environment. One of the most fascinating examples of this coastal specialization is in bottlenose dolphins. The dolphin with which most people are familiar is actually the coastal bottlenose, but we are finding, particularly off the east coast of the US, that there is also an 'offshore' type. The two groups have genetic differences as well as morphological ones; indeed we may be observing the evolution of a new species. The coastal variety has a longer rostrum, more robust pectoral flippers and is slightly smaller; all of these appear to favor life in a shallow-water environment.

The bottlenose dolphin lives in coastal and near-shore waters of much

BOTTLENOSE DOLPHINS

Much uncertainty surrounds the question of how many species of bottlenose dolphin exist. Scientists have 'split' other dolphins (such as common dolphins and spinner dolphins) into several species on the basis of such things as their genetics or where they live, and the same will probably happen with bottlenose dolphins as we learn more about them.

BOTTLENOSE DOLPHINS (right)

HECTOR'S DOLPHINS *(above)*, **DUSKY DOLPHIN** *(right)*
These two, very different, dolphins both live in the coastal waters of New Zealand.

of the world. It is a medium-sized dolphin with adults typically reaching about 8 ft (2.5 m) in length. A great deal is known about this species because it has been studied for many years both in the wild and in captivity, where they live and breed successfully. Because of this wealth of knowledge, many of the generalizations that are made about the delphinids are based on the bottlenose dolphin.

Another of the dolphin species about which a great deal has been learned in the last few years is the Hector's dolphin, *Cephalorhynchus hectori*, which is named for Sir James Hector who was the first curator of the colonial museum in Wellington, New Zealand. Hector's is one of the smallest dolphins, with the adult females, which are larger than the males, reaching only 5 ft (1.5 m). Hector's dolphins are found only in the waters around New Zealand, they live near the coast and show notable site fidelity. The Hector's dolphin is one of the most imperiled of the dolphins with their population numbering only in the hundreds of animals. Fishing operations, by inadvertently killing many dolphins, have significantly impacted the genetic diversity of these animals.

If you've ever traveled between North America and Europe by ship, you've probably seen the white-beaked dolphin, or *Lagenorhynchus*

Fish-Eating or Mammal-Eating Killer Whales

In the Pacific Northwest of the US and Canada, there is a fascinating example of niche specialization in killer whales. Early in the study of these killer whales, researchers noticed two sub-types of killer whales; the first they saw regularly in large groups during the spring, summer and fall, and they dubbed these groups or pods as 'residents'. The second type was more transient, moving through the area of Puget Sound and Vancouver Island in small groups of 1-4 animals, so they called them the 'transients'. As it turns out, the differences between these two groups are substantial and multi-faceted, ranging from what they eat to the sounds they produce. Years of study have shown that the residents eat fish almost exclusively, with most of their diet being salmon. The transients, on the other hand, do not eat fish but instead prey upon other marine mammals, primarily seals, sea lions and small dolphins and porpoises. Based on these dietary differences, the two groups of killer whales are more commonly known now as 'fish-eating' and 'mammal-eating' types. Not only do they travel in different-sized groups, but they use their echolocation system quite differently.

KILLER WHALES

The odontocete echolocation system is discussed in more detail later, but it's interesting to note that the fish-eating killer whales produce echolocation in a very uniform way with the clicks being produced at regular intervals and in discrete trains. The mammal eaters, however, make clicks irregularly and sparingly, producing short bursts of 5-10 clicks, then falling silent, and then producing one or two at erratic intervals. Why, you might ask, wouldn't the mammal-eating whales use their sophisticated echolocation system to its fullest extent? The best explanation for this phenomenon is that their prey can most likely hear their clicks, whereas the prey of the fish eaters cannot, so the mammal eaters would not want to betray their presence to their prey, which would diminish their success in capturing them.

This fascinating difference between the fish- and mammal-eating killer whales is a good example of niche separation, and in fact this separation is apparently being codified in their genetic code, so there may soon be two true sub-species of killer whales.

albirostris. This genus, *Lagenorhynchus*, commonly known as the 'lags', has several representatives, most of which live offshore. The white-beaked dolphin is one of the largest of this genus and indeed one of the largest of the group we typically think of as 'dolphins', though as we mentioned earlier, the dolphin family includes species all the way to the killer whale. The white-beaked dolphin gets its name from the light coloration of its rostrum, and its scientific name, *albirostris*, is a combination of

the Latin *albino* or white and *rostral* or beak. These dolphins primarily inhabit the coasts of the North Atlantic ocean, making their way as far as the icy seas of the Arctic in the summer, though they are not ice-adapted in the same way as the true inhabitants of these waters, like narwhals or beluga whales.

The killer whale, *Orcinus orca*, is the largest of the dolphin family and inhabits virtually every oceanic habitat in the world. Though they are considerably larger than any of their dolphin cousins and have rounded rostrums, which is characteristic of the porpoises; they do have conical-shaped teeth and are genetically part of the dolphin family. Killer whales

KILLER WHALE

Killer whales are one of the most well known species of dolphins, though many people do not realize that they are indeed part of the dolphin family. Killer whales are fascinating in many ways, particularly in their social groupings and their foraging strategies. Socially, they live in matrilineal groups, and remain in these throughout their lives. Some groups specialize in preying on fish and others on mammals.

AMAZON RIVER DOLPHINS

The animal in the foreground is demonstrating one of the many differences between river dolphins and their sea-living cousins – they can turn their heads! This flexibility, combined with broader flippers and pincer-like jaws, allows river dolphins to make a living in the tangled vegetation of the flooded forest.

live very long lives in very tight family groups, typically called pods. The pods are 'matri-focal', which means that an individual whale spends its entire life living in a group with its mother and siblings. When the family of one female becomes too large, they will split into several smaller groups, but remain part of the same pod. Often seen in coastal waters, their range is truly impressive, reaching from the warm waters of the Gulf of Mexico to both the Arctic and Antarctic. Killer whales are the consummate predators, adapted in many ways to prey on fish as well as other marine mammals.

River Dolphins

Some people may be surprised to learn that some dolphins live in rivers. Indeed, some species spend their whole lives in rivers, while other 'river' dolphins do venture into the ocean but never move far from shore. Not surprisingly, these river dolphins possess some significant adaptations that allow them to thrive in this relatively specialized environment. One of the most notable is the presence of a very long rostrum, which they use to pick prey items out of cluttered areas such as tree roots that grow down into the rivers. Another adaptation concerns their poor eyesight. All dolphins possess a sophisticated echolocation system, but the oceanic dolphins do not appear to use it continuously, perhaps suggesting that they can capture prey with vision, passive listening or both. River dolphins depend heavily on echolocation, as they have almost completely lost their ability to see in the murky river waters. Overall, the river dolphins represent a highly specialized group, having adapted to life in a very different environment than that inhabited by their dolphin cousins.

One small member of the river dolphin family is the franciscana dolphin or *Pontoporia blainvillei*. The franciscana spends some time in the rivers of South America, but they also live part of their lives in the coastal waters of northeastern South America. The franciscana is currently a significant conservation concern because of its range. Other river dolphins include the baiji or Chinese river dolphin (*Lipotes vexillifer*), and the boto or Amazon river dolphin (*Inia geoffrensis*), which live in the Yangtze and Amazon rivers, respectively, and spend their whole lives in their rivers.

River dolphins are difficult to study because they are normally quite solitary and skittish around boats. Additionally, river water is often cloudy, which makes observing them even more challenging. Relatively little is known about their life history and ecology. Due to this lack of knowledge and the fact that their range spans many countries, it has been difficult to implement effective conservation measures. There are efforts in South America to create unified international policies on many conservation issues, and hopefully the franciscana will benefit from these efforts.

AMAZON RIVER DOLPHINS

This photo shows two males, which are larger and pinker than females. Often known as the pink dolphin or boto, the Amazon river dolphin is the only member of the group that is still reasonably abundant in most parts of its original range. Its relatives in Asia – occupying the rivers Yangtze, Indus and Ganges – are all heavily impacted by man, and in grave danger of extinction.

A Dolphin's Early Years

To look more closely at the lives of dolphins themselves, it is useful to focus primarily on the bottlenose dolphin, as so much is known about this species, but we will also consider the lives of other species of dolphins along the way. However, from here onward, the name 'dolphin' usually refers to the bottlenose dolphin.

Most of the information known about bottlenose dolphins comes from an ongoing study of the local dolphin population in Sarasota Bay, Florida, which has been carried out for over 35 years, longer even than Jane Goodall's study of chimps. Researchers here have discovered an amazing amount about these dolphins.

Birth to 1 Year

At birth, a baby dolphin is about 3 ft (1 m) in length and weighs around 33 lb (15 kg), and, like many other mammals, they are able to swim from the moment of birth. For many mammals, like deer for example, the ability to walk, swim or run at birth is very important so they can avoid

ATLANTIC SPOTTED DOLPHINS
Young dolphins stay with their mothers for an average of 3-6 years. By age 6 a young dolphin is normally catching its own food. 3-year-olds sometimes leave their mothers due to the arrival of a newborn. When a female gives birth to a new calf older calves are on their own.

BOTTLENOSE DOLPHINS (left)

Dolphin Communication

In addition to the social aspects of growing up within a group of dolphins is the development of a distinctive whistle that occurs during the first months of a dolphin's life. Each dolphin has a unique whistle, a so-called 'signature whistle' that develops early in its life and stays with it for the rest of its life. Dolphins produce many different types of sounds, but the signature whistle is an important part of their repertoire.

Some prominent marine mammal scientists have studied these signature whistles extensively. Initially it was thought these whistles might be related to a dolphin being in a stressful situation; however, the prevalence of signature-whistle use in wild animals demonstrates that they are part of the everyday vocal repertoire. It has been shown that dolphins can mimic each other's signature whistles, an ability that was found to be important as the dolphins use these whistles to maintain contact with each other. Other reaserch showed that signature whistles are very stable, changing very little throughout a dolphin's life, and it was also experimentally demonstrated that individual dolphins show preferences for the signature whistles of animals with which they associate closely.

The link between the whistles to which a calf is exposed during its formative months or years and its final signature whistle has also been investigated. An interesting difference between captive-born and wild dolphins was discovered. The calves born in captivity tended to have more 'flat' parts to their signature whistles than did the wild ones. The term 'flat' refers to the frequency contour or pitch changes that occur during the whistle (see picture). So, the wild animals modulated their whistles a great deal, while the captive ones had more of these flat sections. It seems that the captive animals are most likely influenced by the trainer's whistles, which are simply flat, unmodulated whistles, like a dog whistle, essentially producing a single tone. When the captive dolphins 'constructed' their whistles, they apparently incorporated these flat whistles as part of their own, whereas the wild dolphins had relatively little flat portion in their signature whistles.

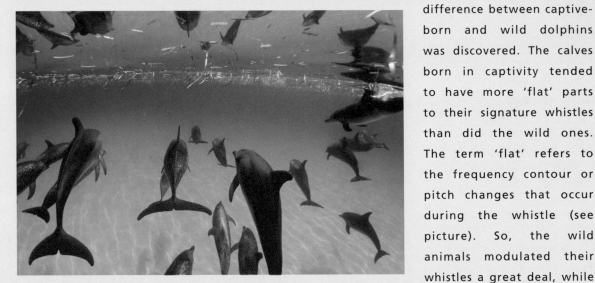

ATLANTIC SPOTTED DOLPHINS

danger. Dolphins, which are preyed upon by sharks, need to be able to swim not only to avoid predation but also to get to the surface to breathe. A baby dolphin's mother will often help it to reach the surface for its first breath by swimming beneath the calf and gently helping it to ascend. Female dolphins with calves are often found together in 'nursery groups'. These groups help to provide protection to the calves. Being in these groups is also important for the socialization of the calf.

Social Groups

Dolphins live in complex societies with hierarchical relationships; in fact many comparisons have been made between dolphin and primate societies, which we know to be quite intricate. To learn about living in such complex social groups requires that the calves be socialized and this process takes place as they live with their mothers in groups of dolphins that vary in size and composition.

Dolphin groups, like chimpanzee societies, are sometimes called 'fission-fusion', meaning that the composition of a group is very fluid as members leave and join. Female dolphins can often be found with their female calves, but the males are less often seen with their mothers, unlike killer whales which spend their whole lives with their mothers and her other offspring. While male dolphins do not spend much time with their

ATLANTIC SPOTTED DOLPHINS

After leaving their mothers, young dolphins are often seen alone or in small groups. As they move into the juvenile stage, however, they are often in larger groups, socializing with other juveniles. These social groups can be thrilling to watch as the dolphins perform aerial and acoustic acrobatics. Indeed, the sounds produced by these socializing groups are exciting and varied.

RISSO'S DOLPHINS

Young dolphins, particularly newborns, can usually be found swimming in 'calf position', which is just next to the mother's flank. In this position the calf can actually glide on the mother's wake, thereby saving some energy. Being so close to its mother also allows the calf to stay in tactile contact so it can accelerate, turn, or dive just when its mother does, which is important for it to avoid being separated.

mothers after they are weaned, older offspring often return for a 'visit' when a new calf is born. So, a baby dolphin is exposed to its siblings during its first few years, with more time being spent on the whole with its female siblings.

Weaning

Dolphin calves nurse for varying lengths of time depending on the species. Most will suckle for at least a year though some will take milk for up to three years. In a study of captive bottlenose dolphin calves, all of them began to eat solid food within a year of birth, although suckling continued for 14 to 37 months after birth. Data from spotted dolphins indicate that calves begin to take solid food at approximately 6 months of age, or 45 in (115 cm), but continue to suckle until they are nearly 2 years old. Interestingly, calves tended to feed more frequently on squid as they aged, suggesting a shift in diet during weaning. The average age and total body length at weaning was estimated to be approximately 9 months and 48 in (122 cm). The oldest suckling calf was almost 2 years old, which suggests that some calves continued to suckle for more than a year after they could have been weaned.

Motherhood

One study conducted in Florida directly addressed questions of the 'parenting' skills of inexperienced an experienced mothers. Research has shown that very few first-born calves survive, and some females have had to try three to four times before successfully raising a calf to weaning. There are probably several reasons for this pattern.

One possibility is that first-born calves bear the brunt of the load of toxic chemicals that have built up in a female's body over her years up to giving birth. Many human activities, including simple things like fertilizing the lawn, result in toxic chemicals being released into the oceans, and these chemicals can be particularly concentrated close to shore where they first enter the ocean. Dolphins, as top predators, can receive significant doses of these chemicals from the fish they eat, and these chemicals are often deposited in their blubber or other fat reserves. Producing milk requires a great deal of energy for females and one energy reserve is the lipids in their blubber. So, when these females start making milk for the first time, these chemicals are 'mobilized' and passed along to their calves. The first calf would theoretically receive the largest dose of chemicals because its mother has been accumulating them over her whole life.

Another possible reason that first and often second calves do not survive may well be due to the level of their mother's parenting expertise. Some years ago, a study was undertaken of the behavioral differences between first-time and experienced mothers. The study looked at things like distance and position of mother and calf at each surfacing, proximity of mother-calf pairs to other groups, and composition of nearby groups. What was found was quite interesting in that first-time mothers were more likely to let their calves stray farther from them and the calves did not surface in 'calf position' nearly as often. Additionally, these 'inexperienced' mothers spent less time in groups with other females and/or mother-calf pairs. While it is not possible to draw direct conclusions about the relationship between these behavioral patterns and survival rates of calves because of the other factors involved, some of the data do point to greater survival success for calves raised by mothers who are more vigilant about their calves and their surroundings.

INDO-PACIFIC HUMP-BACKED DOLPHINS

As is true for all mammals, producing milk to feed young is energetically demanding for females. Food consumption in some captive dolphins showed little increase during gestation, but was 58-97 percent higher during lactation than during similar periods in non-reproductive years. In addition to higher food consumption, some female dolphins have also shown a change in their diet to more calorie-rich foods compared to those they eat when they are not lactating.

HAWAIIAN SPINNER DOLPHINS

Dolphins are born precocial, which means they start swimming as soon as they are born; so they can get to the surface to breathe, avoid predators, and keep up with their mothers. Their mothers may have to help the newborns to the surface the first time to breathe, but then they swim on their own.

BOTTLENOSE DOLPHINS (right)

During their first year, calves spend most of their time in close proximity to their mothers. Late in their first year and then increasingly over years two to three, they begin to range farther away. Current research reveals that they do not venture too far yet, and still stay within 550-1100 yds (500-1000 m) of their mothers. There is certainly a good deal of variation here, including what appears to be the 'parenting style' of individual females. At this stage young dolphins can now be seen socializing with older, larger animals, which sometimes includes elder siblings. Occasionally small dolphins are even seen being thrown from the water during these playful social events.

1 to 5 Years

When they are about one year old, young dolphins are often seen spending more and more time away from their mothers, though 1-2 year olds are often still in the immediate area. As these youngsters begin to gain their independence during their first 3 years, they socialize with groups of calves as well as adults that are not their mothers or siblings. With this increasing social independence, however, also comes the need to become nutritionally independent. Young animals continue to nurse for several years, but they begin to take solid food sometime after their first birthday.

DUSKY DOLPHIN

Some dolphin species are famous for their exuberant above-water behavior, both in young and old animals. Dusky dolphins are among the best of these, often leaping high in the air, and the activity is infectious, sometimes resulting in the entire pod apparently in the air at the same time.

Learning to Feed

Catching fish is not an easy task for a dolphin. Most of the fish upon which dolphins prey are fast, agile swimmers that are able to turn and accelerate faster than dolphins, on a relative scale anyway. Dolphins grab prey in their long, tooth-studded jaws and then swallow them whole, except in the case of catfish, which they first decapitate by vigorously shaking them. A 660 lb (300 kg) dolphin chasing a 1 lb (0.5 kg) fish, trying to grab it with its 11 in (30 cm) jaw, is a bit like trying to catch a fly with chopsticks. Suffice to say that dolphins must be extremely quick to be successful. They are also quite creative and resourceful, displaying behaviors that increase their chances of detecting, chasing and finally catching their prey.

These strategies, or foraging behaviors, can be quite spectacular to see, and it is in these years between 2-4 that young dolphins must learn to chase and catch those fish that are swimming for their lives. It is quite likely that young dolphins learn specific foraging behaviors from their mothers or other close associates. Consider one of these spectacular behaviors, the 'fish whack'. As the name implies, the dolphins whack the fish with their tail flukes, often sending the fish 30 ft (10 m) or more through the air. Observations indicate that dolphins usually use this behavior when they encounter a school of fish, so while it might be a bonus to actually hit one of the fish, the behavior may just serve to fracture the school and disorient one or more fish, making them easier targets.

Interestingly, killer whales have been observed executing a similar behavior. What's fascinating is that while there are reports of dolphins using fish-whacking behavior in several locations, not all the animals actually use it. This indicates that there is some specialization occurring, and also the animals that do use it are related and/or spend much of

BOTTLENOSE DOLPHIN

This young bottlenose dolphin is in the process of eating a fish it has just captured. The ready availability of fish is important in the early years of a calf's development, and many youngsters fail to survive the transition to independence. Weaning often occurs when the mother becomes pregnant with her next offspring, at which time she is less receptive to the demands of the juvenile by her side.

Photo-Identification

How do we know one dolphin from another? We use their dorsal fins; like a face or fingerprint, they have distinctive features, even at birth, e.g., shape, size. As the animals age, their fins acquire unique marks, nicks and notches, which make them even easier to identify. Photo-identification is a useful method for tracking individuals, and by photographing all dolphins seen at a particular time and place (a 'sighting'), we can also monitor their association patterns. Once you have photographed animals at a sighting, you can match those fins to ones previously seen in different locations, seasons, or groups.

their time together. Such transmission of specialized behaviors also occurs in other mammals, such as chimps. What researchers are just starting to investigate is the mechanism by which these behaviors are passed from dolphin to dolphin.

Another specialized behavior, the 'kerplunk', may provide a good case study for this transmission. Dolphins in Sarasota and several other places display this behavior. The animal will raise its flukes out of the water and then forcefully bring them back down, splashing at the surface but also continuing the motion right down into the water. This action creates at least two results: a relatively loud 'boom' underwater, and a bubble cloud, both of which could theoretically startle and/or corral fish. Fish like to seek refuge in sea grass beds, and when they are nestled down in the grass it is probably hard for a dolphin to see or echolocate on them. The boom from the kerplunk may well cause a startle reaction in the fish, and when they move they become much easier for the dolphin to detect. Whatever the exact function, an adult female has been observed parading along the edge of a sea grass bed 'kerplunking', followed just about 15 ft (5 m) behind her by her calf, doing the same thing. This has also happened with one female, nicknamed 'Pecan sandie', with two of her calves, separated by about 5 years.

Adolescence

Many of the dolphins in Sarasota Bay, Florida were local residents, with some animals being observed in the area from birth to death. The dolphins most certainly travel outside of the immediate area, but nonetheless year-round surveys document the strong residency patterns of many animals. We do see immigration and emigration in this so-called 'population', although the functional unit in these dolphins really defies definition. The term 'pod' is often used for whales and dolphins, but this has become associated more with the species that spend most of their time with the same animals, like killer whales. The dolphins of Sarasota Bay research area exist in a society with frequent changes in group size and composition. The 120 or so dolphins most frequently seen there are referred to as a 'community', and this community is loosely based on geography, with differences in habitat-use patterns occurring seasonally. This community of animals blends with adjacent groups or communities in some 15 percent of sightings, though recent genetic evidence indicates long-term differentiation between the communities.

How does a young dolphin become part of this relatively closed population? We know that they spend several years in close association with their mother, and then, depending on their mother's experience and her own social grouping, a young dolphin spends its first few years associated with a relatively small number of individuals. As these

ATLANTIC SPOTTED DOLPHINS

One advantage of living in a group is the ability to share food found by others. These spotted dolphins have probably used echolocation to locate fish buried in the sand, and others are coming over to see what the excitement is about. Vision is important in such crystal-clear water, but many dolphins rely almost entirely on sound to learn about what is happening around them.

PACIFIC WHITE-SIDED DOLPHINS

The intense sociality of marine dolphins is apparent in these photographs of Pacific white-sided and common dolphins. From birth and throughout life, a dolphin will rarely, if ever, be alone. In most species, though, group membership is fluid and changes to some extent day by day. The most notable exception to this pattern is the killer whale, whose family groups are often stable for years.

LONG-BEAKED COMMON DOLPHINS (right)

youngsters move into adolescence and later adulthood, they associate with increasing numbers of animals. As adolescents, though, they spend much of their time with other 'sub-adult' animals, and their days are spent primarily feeding and socializing. Studies with captive dolphins have shown that there are definite dominance hierarchies, so it is reasonable to assume that much of dolphin adolescence is spent vying for positions in these hierarchies. Studies of captive dolphins show that, in general, males are dominant over females, possibly due to their larger size. How important male over female dominance is in wild adult dolphins is unknown. Hierarchies within female groups, however, could be quite important as they will potentially spend much of the rest of their lives associating with a relatively small number of other females.

A young female dolphin becomes mature, which is defined as being able to reproduce, at somewhere between 5-10 years of age, and when she has her first calf she begins to spend more and more time with other adult females rather than with the adolescent males and females. Males mature a bit later, though the definition of when a male becomes 'mature' is sometimes different than for females. Males may not successfully sire a calf until around 20 years of age, but it is likely that they are capable of becoming fathers long before that.

Adulthood

The two primary motivations in the life of an adult dolphin, indeed the priorities for most animals, are to find food and to reproduce. For females this means finding suitable mates, breeding and then raising their young. They spend much of their time with other females and their calves. Males, on the other hand, have a much different adult life than females.

Male Alliances

Most male dolphins will, as they become mature, pair up with another adult male, forming an

alliance that often lasts for many years, sometimes for the rest of their lives. These 'male pairs' represent one of the most stable associations we see in dolphins. In fact, the proportion of time they spend together, often called their 'coefficient of association', is well over 90 percent, a figure that is rivaled only by females and young calves. By 'associated' we mean that these males are rarely more than a few hundred yards apart and often swim side-by-side. We do not know a great deal about how the alliance is formed, but once it has, it is unusual to see one male without

SPINNER DOLPHINS

As male dolphins age, they often pair up with another male; this pair bond becomes very strong, with the two spending most of their time together. Pairing up with another male may increase a dolphin's mating opportunities and provide additional protection from predators.

BOTTLENOSE DOLPHINS (left)

COMMERSON'S DOLPHINS

One of the most beautiful and charismatic of all dolphins, this tiny species can sometimes be seen surfing waves in the Falkland Islands, or chasing prey in kelp forests of southern South America. It is one of just four diminutive members of the family Cephalorhynchus, *all of which favor coastal habitats in the southern hemisphere.*

SPINNER DOLPHINS (right)

his buddy. Male pairs are sometimes, though not always, close in age, and occasionally we see a rather old dolphin paired with a youngster. This latter circumstance often results from the death of the older dolphin's longtime partner and then he pairs up with a younger, unpaired male.

Three primary ideas have been offered to explain the existence and possible functions of this social system. The first is that having a full-time buddy might provide protection from predators, by both having an 'extra set of eyes' as well as for actually fending off attacks.

Another possible explanation for the formation and stability of these pair bonds is to increase foraging success through prey detection and/or other cooperative strategies. Finally, the ability to gain access to females could be assisted by working in pairs. Some studies exploring this last hypothesis has yielded some fascinating results. There are significant differences between single males and those in stable alliances in both behavior and physiology. Behaviorally, during the spring and summer mating season, alliance males were observed to maintain association with receptive females for longer periods of time than were single, or 'non-alliance', males. Additionally, these males were observed to be in closer proximity to these females. It is not known exactly what it means to males to maintain prolonged, close association with a female, but the educated guess is that the longer a male (or males) is able to sequester or guard a female from other males and mate with her, the better the chance that he will successfully sire a calf.

Other research explored elements of 'female choice' in dolphins. What is meant by female choice is that the female somehow evaluates the quality of a male (she wants the 'best' male to sire her calf so it can be successful), and then has some means of exercising her choice. As part of this female choice study, females were observed trying to 'escape' from males by swimming rapidly away. So if two males are working together to sequester a female, the assumption is that they will be more successful in doing so, as well as being better at guarding that female from being stolen by another male or pair of males.

Alliance males are not only able to maintain close associations with females for longer periods, but they also enjoy some physical advantages over the non-alliance males. As part of the health assessment work with dolphins in the Sarasota

Male Pair Signature Whistles

Dolphins possess individually distinctive signature whistles with which they can maintain contact and identify close associates. Sometimes the whistles of each male of a pair will slowly change, with each dolphin incorporating features of his buddy's whistle until they converge on a unique 'pair whistle'. The function of a pair whistle has not yet been demonstrated, but given the reproductive advantages that we know result from alliance formation, their shared whistle may have some function in the mating system. A male pair that has demonstrated its dominance would benefit from having a unified signal, as its use may preclude the need for further confrontation. Settling disputes before physical contact can be advantageous for one or both males, because a less competitive male can avoid injury or death by yielding to a dominant animal without having to engage in physical contact.

Florida research area, we have learned that alliance males are bulkier than non-alliance males during the mating season, that is to say they actually put on weight in the spring and summer, which would theoretically make them more competitive with other males when trying to maintain access to females. Additionally, the testosterone levels of alliance males are higher than they are in non-alliance males during this period.

These differences in behavior and physiology are certainly fascinating, but to truly link them to increased mating success we need to know that these alliance males are siring more calves than non-alliance males.

Genetic studies of the Sarasota dolphins have indeed proved this fact. Therefore, alliance formation in male dolphins does confer a reproductive advantage. Interestingly this alliance formation is found in dolphins in other parts of the world. In Shark Bay, Western Australia, alliances are common, and in fact alliances of three instead of two males are also observed. Another feature of this Shark Bay system is the formation of 'super alliances', in which two or more male alliances will join forces in apparent competition with other super alliances, presumably for access to females.

The Search for Food

In addition to finding mates, adult dolphins must also find food for themselves. Dolphins in Florida's Sarasota Bay eat a variety of things, primarily fish. Our knowledge of what precisely they eat is based primarily on exploring the stomach contents of dolphins that die and are recovered. To name a few, these dolphins eat pinfish, pigfish, mullet, cat fish, jacks, and toadfish. Ongoing studies of fish distribution and ecology are exploring whether dolphins prey upon fish in direct relationship to the abundance of those fish, i.e., do they just eat what is most plentiful?

How they find and capture their prey is one area of particular interest. Dolphins and the rest of the toothed whales possess a sophisticated echolocation system. The term 'echolocation' is quite descriptive; a dolphin produces a short burst of sound energy, a so-called 'click', that travels out through the water, bounces off some target (e.g., fish, seawall), and the echo travels back to the dolphin. Upon receiving the echo the dolphin is able to learn something about the target due to characteristics of the echo, specifically the way(s) in which the target has changed that signal. The characteristics of the outgoing click are presumably well known by the dolphin, and the unique properties of the target uniquely alter the signal. The changes to the signal (e.g., amplitude and frequency), as well as the time required for the click to travel to the target and back, are then processed by the

BOTTLENOSE DOLPHINS

Catching fish is often easier for a dolphin when it is in a group rather than alone. Fish tend to 'bunch' together when threatened from several directions at once or frightened by lots of noise in the water, and are easier to track when there is help from other hungry dolphins. Sometimes, dolphins simply play with fish, in the same way that a cat does with a mouse – catching and releasing it several times before it dies of stress or damage.

ATLANTIC SPOTTED DOLPHINS (left)

LONG-BEAKED COMMON DOLPHINS
The water fills with excited whistles and echolocation clicks when dolphins corral their prey.

dolphin to give it information about the location and nature of the target. Suffice to say that the system is impressively sophisticated and can provide detailed information about the targets. Though it is very difficult to record clicks produced by wild, foraging dolphins, we believe that they do indeed use their echolocation system to detect and locate their prey.

Echolocation is considered to be an 'active' hunting system as opposed to a 'passive' one because the predator is actually producing a signal that could theoretically be detected by its prey. Compare this with a predator that hunts exclusively with vision or smell. The predator does not produce any signal, except its mere presence, that could be detected by its prey. Echolocating animals like dolphins and many bats, however, actually produce sounds that their prey, if properly equipped, could sense, therefore betraying the presence of the predator and then presumably making it easier for the prey to escape.

Decades of research have shown that the prey of echolocating bats do indeed detect and respond to the signals of their predators, and they even employ several fascinating countermeasures. The prey of dolphins has not been investigated as extensively, but it is known that some species of fishes possess the ability to hear sounds that are well out of the range in which they produce their own signals. The most plausible explanation for this hearing sensitivity is to enable fish to detect echolocating predators, though there is no experimental evidence that they do this in the wild. As a potential countermeasure to this hearing ability, however, it has been found that dolphins do respond to sounds

BOTTLENOSE DOLPHIN

One of the most important things dolphins do is search for and find food. The behavioral strategies they employ are impressive and fascinating. These foraging behaviors range from simple acceleration, to 'pinwheels', which are like a swimmer's flip turn, to the 'fish whack'. This behavior consists of a dolphin striking one or more fish with its tail flukes, with fish often flying up to 30 ft (10 m) through the air! The above dolphin is using echolocation to locate prey buried beneath the sand.

BOTTLENOSE DOLPHINS

This edition published in 2006 by Voyageur Press, an imprint of MBI Publishing Company,
Galtier Plaza, Suite 200, 380 Jackson Street, St. Paul, MN 55101-3885 USA

ISBN-13: 978-0-7603-2561-2   ISBN-10: 0-7603-2561-8
Printed in China

Front cover: ATLANTIC SPOTTED DOLPHIINS;
Back cover: COMMON DOLPHINS;   Page 1: BOTTLENOSE DOLPHINS

BIOGRAPHY: **Stephanie Nowacek** gained an M.Sc. in Marine Science from the
University of California, Santa Cruz. She is currently the Lab. Manager for the Sarasota
Dolphin Research Project in Florida.

Dr. Douglas Nowacek holds a Ph.D. in Biological Oceanography from MIT- Woods Hole
Oceanographic Institution Joint Program. He is Assistant Professor in the Department of
Oceanography at Florida State University.

Photographs © 2006 by:

Andy Rouse (NHPA): 38

Christopher Swann: 12

Colin Baxter: 7, 15, 25

Carlos Eyles/SeaPics.com: 23

Doug Perrine/SeaPics.com: Front cover, 1, 22, 31,
34, 37, 43, 44, 45

Fernando Trujillo/SeaPics.com: 20

Francois Gohier: 8, 11, 14, 19, 39, 40, back cover

Gregory Ochocki/SeaPics.com: 21

Hiroya Minakuchi/SeaPics.com: 17, 32

Horoto Kawaguchi/ephotography/SeaPics.com: 29

Ingrid Visser/SeaPics.com: 2, 16, 18, 33, 48

James D. Watt/SeaPics.com: 5, 42, 46

Kike Calvo/SeaPics.com: 26

Laurie Campbell: 4

Masa Ushioda/SeaPics.com: 10, 30, 41

Michael S. Nolan/SeaPics.com: 6, 28

Phillip Colla/SeaPics.com: 35

Randy Morse/SeaPics.com: 36

Robert L. Pitman/SeaPics.com: 9, 13

Thomas Jefferson/SeaPics.com: 27

Tim Calver/SeaPics.com: 24

Todd Pusser: 47